FIRST AMERICANS

The Nez Perce

DAVID C. KING

Marshall Cavendish
Benchmark
New York

J970.1
Kin

ACKNOWLEDGMENTS

Series consultant: Raymond Bial

The words of Chief Joseph quoted on page 18 are from an interview with him: "An Indian's View of Indian Affairs."
North American Review 128:269 (April 1879): 412–33

Marshall Cavendish Benchmark
99 White Plains Road
Tarrytown, New York 10591-9001
www.marshallcavendish.us

Text copyright © 2008 by Marshall Cavendish Corporation
Map and illustrations copyright © 2008 by Marshall Cavendish Corporation.
Maps and illustrations by Rodica Prato
Craft illustrations by Chris Santoro

Library of Congress Cataloging-in-Publication Data
King, David C.
  The Nez Perce / by David C. King.
       p. cm. — (First Americans)
  Summary: "Provides comprehensive information on the background, lifestyle, beliefs, and present-day lives of the Nez Perce people"—Provided by publisher.
  Includes bibliographical references and index.
  ISBN-13: 978-0-7614-2680-6
  1. Nez Perce Indians—Juvenile literature.   I. Title. II. Series.
  E99.N5K56 2007
  979.6004'974124—dc22
2006034114

On the cover: A Nez Perce boy from Idaho in tribal costume
Title page: An example of Nez Perce beadwork

Photo research by Connie Gardner
Cover photo by Kike Calvo © Visuals and Written SL/Alamy
Title Page by Glenn Oakley/Idaho Stock Image
SuperStock: Kent and Charlene Krone, 4; Prisma, 35. Corbis: 38, W. Wayne Lockwood, 6; Historical Picture Archive, 8; Edward S. Curtis, 12; Kit Houghton, 18; Macduff Everton, 36; Kevin R. Morris, 39. Nativetock.com: Marilyn "Angel" Wynn, 9, 20, 23, 24, 32, 33, 41. Raymond Bial: 16. NorthWind Picture Archive: 21. Art Resource: HIP, 25. Alamy: Chuck Place, 28. Bridgeman Art Library: Stapleton Collection, 30. AP Photo: Don Ryan, 40.

Editor: Deborah Grahame
Publisher: Michelle Bisson
Editorial Director: Michelle Bisson
Art Director: Anahid Hamparian
Series designer: Symon Chow

Printed in China
1 3 5 6 4 2

CONTENTS

1 • Who Are the Nez Perce People?   5

2 • How the Nez Perce Lived   17

3 • Nez Perce Beliefs   29

4 • A Changing World   37

Time Line   42
Glossary   44
Find Out More   46
Index   48

1 · WHO ARE THE NEZ PERCE PEOPLE?

For most of their history, the Nez Perce (Nez PURSE) have lived in a rugged area of what is now the state of Idaho. This is a beautiful, hilly land, where bright streams flow out of the Bitterroot Mountains into fast-moving rivers, such as the Clearwater and the Salmon.

The Nez Perce people have been known by many different names. They first called themselves the *Nimi'ipuu* (Nee-mee-poo). Then, in the early 1800s, French-Canadian traders called them the *Nez Perce*, a French term meaning "pierced nose." The term referred to a nose ornament some of the Nez Perce wore. The name stuck, even though only a few of the people wore the decoration.

Over the past three hundred years, the way of life of the Nez Perce has changed several times. First, in the early 1700s,

The Bitterroot Mountains in Idaho.

Range ponies, including chestnut, pinto, bay, and roan.

the villagers in the eastern portion of the Nez Perce lands learned about horses. Spanish soldiers and explorers had brought the first horses to North America in the early 1500s. Some of the horses had escaped and roamed free across the huge grasslands called the **Great Plains**, which stretch from Mexico to Canada. Over the next two hundred years, the wild horses had multiplied into large herds.

American Indian tribes living on the Great Plains soon learned to tame the wild horses and became skilled riders. The swift horses helped them to become expert hunters and feared warriors.

Some young Nez Perce from the eastern villages visited people of the Sioux tribe on the Plains. The Sioux taught them to be skilled at hunting on horseback. The Sioux and other Plains tribes mostly hunted buffalo for food and for its hide, used for clothing and shelter. Huge herds of these big, shaggy beasts shared the grasslands with the Indians and the wild horses.

Leading bands of tamed horses, the Nez Perce went back to their villages and spread the word about an exciting new way of life on the Great Plains. Beginning in the 1700s more and more of the Nez Perce left their villages for half the year to follow the buffalo herds. Some, especially in the western part of Nez Perce lands, chose to remain in their riverside villages.

On the Great Plains, the Nez Perce bands, with several families in each, followed the buffalo herds through spring, summer, and fall. The hunters rode alongside the herd on their swift horses and used bows and arrows and short spears to bring down the thousand-pound (454-kilogram) beasts. The women then cut up the buffalo. In addition to the meat, they used nearly every other part of the animal. Hunting bands lived in cone-shaped tents called **tipis.** As winter

Hunting buffalo on the Great Plains. Later, the use of rifles made the hunters even more successful.

approached, the bands returned to their traditional settlements in the river valleys.

The Nez Perce prospered as buffalo hunters. They became experts at raising and training **Appaloosa** horses. By about 1800 they had one of the largest Appaloosa herds in North America. They also had become one of the most powerful tribes in the western half of the United States.

The Nez Perce faced more changes in the 1800s. American explorers Meriwether Lewis and William Clark traveled through their lands in 1805. A few years later, French-Canadian and American fur trappers arrived. They hunted and trapped beaver for their fur. Christian missionaries came next, and converted many of the people to Christianity.

A missionary with Nez Perce on a reservation.

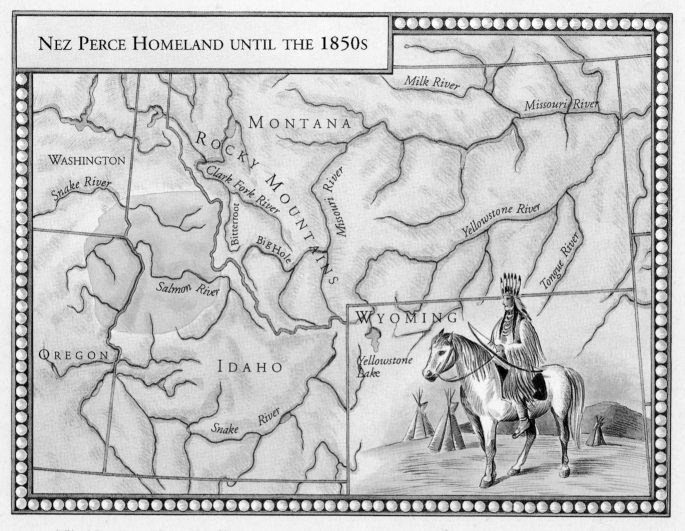

NEZ PERCE HOMELAND UNTIL THE 1850s

Milk River

Missouri River

MONTANA

ROCKY MOUNTAINS

WASHINGTON

Snake River

Clark Fork River

Bitterroot

Big Hole

Missouri River

Yellowstone River

Tongue River

Salmon River

OREGON

IDAHO

WYOMING

Yellowstone Lake

Snake River

The Nez Perce homeland was centered in what became the state of Idaho.

Around 1840 wagon trains began to rumble across Nez Perce lands on the way to the fertile farmland of Oregon and California. In an effort to make peace between the American pioneers and the Indians, officials of the U.S. government called for a meeting with several tribes. Although many young warriors wanted to fight the settlers and the soldiers, Nez Perce leaders agreed to sign a treaty in 1855. The treaty created a large **reservation** that covered most of the traditional Nez Perce lands.

At first, calling their land a reservation did not seem to make much difference in the lives of the people. Then, five years later, an American miner named Elias Pierce discovered gold on the Snake and Clearwater rivers on the Nez Perce reservation. Almost immediately, thousands of miners swarmed over Nez Perce lands. Instead of protecting reservation lands as outlined in the Treaty of 1855, U.S. officials forced the Nez Perce chiefs to sign a new treaty in 1863. In this treaty they were instructed to give up three-quarters of their land.

Many of the Nez Perce refused to accept the new treaty and to move onto the smaller reservation. The warriors who had wanted to resist the earlier treaty now began raiding settlements, killing people, and burning down settlers' cabins. The settlers responded with raids on Nez Perce villages. The fighting dragged on for several years.

In 1877 the federal

Chief Joseph of the Nez Perce in a 1903 photograph.

government sent the U.S. Army to force the Nez Perce onto their reservation. Chief Joseph, a young leader of the tribe, agreed to lead his band onto the reservation. He had opposed both treaties, but he also knew that he could not resist the powerful U.S. Army. Years of warfare already had cost the lives of many of his people. As his band prepared to move, however, Chief Joseph learned that Nez Perce warriors had killed several settlers. Fearing that they would be blamed for the deaths, Chief Joseph and other leaders decided to flee from the soldiers.

The surrender of Chief Joseph brought an end to what is known as the Nez Perce War. Many of the Nez Perce were sent to a reservation in present-day Oklahoma, where they became ill with malaria and other diseases. Many died far from their traditional home in Idaho. In 1885 the survivors were finally moved to a reservation in Washington State, but they were never allowed to return to the land of their ancestors.

The Flight of the Nez Perce

Chief Joseph and other Nez Perce leaders, fearing an attack by the U.S. Army, decided to try to escape, first to Montana and then to Canada. With about two hundred warriors and five hundred others, mostly women and children, the Nez Perce began their frantic march in July 1877. The army, led by General Howard, gave chase.

Day after day, the Nez Perce trudged on. Time and again the pursuing soldiers seemed to have them trapped, but the Nez Perce used clever tactics to fight their way out. They made their way through the rugged Bitterroot Mountains into Montana. As winter closed in, however, they found themselves trapped just 40 miles (64 kilometers) short of the Canadian border. They had avoided the army for three months while covering 1,700 miles (2,736 km) through Oregon, Wyoming, Idaho, and Montana. American newspapers had followed the story, and people cheered the courageous Nez Perce.

When he surrendered on October 5, 1877, Chief Joseph gave one of the great speeches in American history. Speaking through an interpreter, he described the great tragedy of his people. He ended with these famous words: "Hear me, my Chiefs: I am tired. My heart is sick and sad. From where the sun now stands, I will fight no more forever."

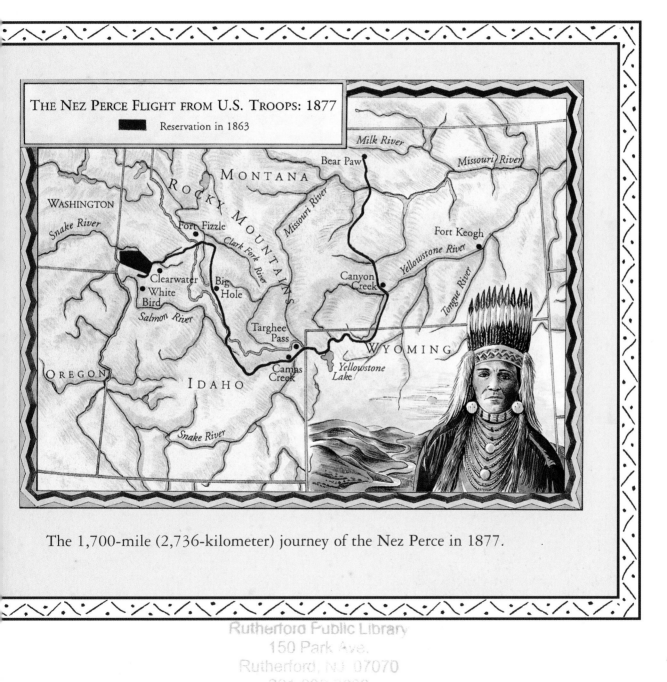

The 1,700-mile (2,736-kilometer) journey of the Nez Perce in 1877.

2 · HOW THE NEZ PERCE LIVED

A young boy proudly rode a horse into a Nez Perce village. Almost twenty cone-shaped tipis were clustered on the banks of a narrow stream. The boy was proud because he had broken a wild horse by himself. The spirited little horse had thrown him several times before it finally settled down and allowed him to ride.

Adding a new horse to the herd was important to the Nez Perce. They depended on their horses for hunting, transportation, and warfare. The Nez Perce were famous for their breeding of horses, especially the beautiful spotted horses known as Appaloosas. They sold some of the horses at American trading posts in exchange for things they could not make themselves, such as rifles, iron kettles, metal tools, and some factory-made clothes.

A Nez Perce tipi.

The Nez Perce and the Appaloosa

No other tribe had horse herds as large as the Nez Perce. They were best known for their handsome Appaloosa horses. The name came from the Palouse River in the heart of Nez Perce territory. The name now also refers to the horses' coloring, which is usually a gray or cream with many tan spots, or another color with white spots.

The spotted coat of an Appaloosa pony.

The Appaloosa herds helped make the Nez Perce one of the most prosperous Indian tribes. They hoped that prosperity would help them remain independent. In 1873, when the Nez Perce refused to move onto a smaller reservation, Chief Joseph said,

We are contented and happy if the white man will let us alone. The reservation is too small for so many people with all their stock…. We have plenty of horses and cattle to sell, and we won't have any help from you. We are free now. We can go where we please. Our fathers were born here. Here they lived, here they died, here are their graves. We will never leave them.

[From the Report of the Secretary of the Interior, 1872–1873]

Horses allowed the Nez Perce to pursue an exciting way of life: hunting buffalo on the Great Plains. About half the tribe's fifty bands moved onto the grasslands to follow the huge herds through spring, summer, and fall.

The people moved their hunting camps several times during the season to keep close to a herd. Tipis were taken down and carried on the sturdy backs of the horses. To carry supplies, the Nez Perce used the **travois** (truh-VOY). Other goods were carried in saddlebags.

When the north winds turned cold and brought the first hint of winter snow, the Nez Perce on the Great Plains packed up their belongings and moved to the high country, where some of the bands chose to remain all year. The way of life was quite different in the river valleys of the mountains. Instead of building tipis, the people lived in sturdy lodges made of wooden poles that leaned toward the center, forming an A-shaped frame that was covered with woven mats. The lodges were narrow and long. As many as thirty families could live in the largest lodges. Several cooking fires were placed in the center, and each was shared by at least two families. A hole in the roof mats allowed most of the smoke to escape, but some smoke still lingered in the dim lodges.

The main food in the mountain valleys was salmon, rather than buffalo meat. People caught salmon in nets or with three-pronged fishing spears. There was plenty of salmon, and it was easily caught. Villagers dried the fish on wooden racks and then stored it in pits for winter use. Every village also had a wooded area for hunting. They allowed other villages to hunt there, too, usually for deer.

A Nez Perce lodge covered with woven mats.

The Nez Perce found many wild foods that gave them a varied and healthy diet. There were many kinds of wild berries, including blue-berries and blackberries. The people used digging sticks with cross handles made of antler to harvest roots. The bulb of the **camas** was the favorite. Other roots included **couse**, wild car-rot, onion, and parsnips.

Some of the cooking was done in pits lined with hot stones. Villagers also roasted meat on sticks over an open fire or hung a skin bag from a wooden frame and piled hot stones

Catching salmon on the Columbia River.

Fruit Leather

The Nez Perce ate a food similar to this tasty dried fruit, especially when they traveled. They dried mashed fruit in the sun. Ask an adult to help you with this recipe.

You will need the following ingredients and equipment:

- 2 to 3 cups mixed fresh fruit (use soft fruits such as grapes, berries, peaches, or apricots)
- kitchen strainer
- table knife or paring knife

- electric blender
- cookie sheet
- plastic wrap or wax paper
- wooden mixing spoon
- container with lid

1. Wash the fruit and drain it. Leave the skins on.
2. Use a table knife to cut the fruit into small pieces.
3. Place the fruit in a blender and pulse on high for 15 seconds.
4. Line a cookie sheet with plastic wrap or wax paper.
5. Spread the fruit mixture onto the lined cookie sheet. Place it in a warm place for about 24 hours.
6. To preserve the fruit leather, roll up the plastic wrap and store it in a covered container. Do not refrigerate. To eat the leather, simply unroll the wrap and peel off as much as you want. Your fruit leather can be stored for up to 2 weeks.

under it. Fresh buffalo meat was cut into strips and hung on wooden racks to dry into a chewy treat called **jerky**. Some of the jerky was pounded into a powder and mixed with either bone marrow or dried berries to make **pemmican**.

The women made clothing out of **buckskin** (softened deerskin) or buffalo hide. In winter, people wrapped themselves in buffalo robes. Men wore leggings made of rabbit fur, and women wore leggings of woven hemp fiber. Everyone wore moccasins made of buffalo hide. Men wore headbands, and on the Plains they made feathered war bonnets.

Drying buffalo meat for jerky or pemmican.

Nez Perce War Bonnet

When the Nez Perce began following the buffalo herds on the Great Plains, they copied many of the ways of other Plains Indians, such as the Sioux and the Blackfoot. One of the patterns they copied was the Indian war bonnet, or headdress. A warrior added a feather to his headband for each feat that his tribal council approved. If the headband was filled with feathers, more were added down the back.

You will need:

- 3-inch-wide strip of flexible cardboard, long enough to fit around your head plus 1 to 2 inches
- 2 sheets of white paper
- pencil
- scissors
- crayons
- 6 or 7 cotton balls
- stapler
- glue

1· Measure the cardboard strip to fit around your head, with an overlap of 1 to 2 inches. Use crayons to decorate the band with geometric designs.

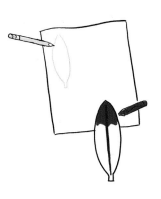

2· Draw a feather pattern. Cut it out and use it as a pattern to make 10 or 11 more.

3· Use a dark brown crayon to color the tip of the feather and to draw lines down the center, as shown.

4· Place the feathers evenly along the headband, and staple or glue them in place. To imitate the Indians' use of the fluff on an eagle's tail feathers, tear cotton balls in half and glue them to the base of each feather. See drawing.

5· Carefully close the headband—remember the overlap—and staple it closed.

Colored beads create the design on these moccasins.

Nez Perce children learned by watching their parents and working alongside them. Boys usually made small bows to use until they were about twelve years old. They learned to make arrows with stone points, which were attached with wet strips of hide that tightened as they dried. When they were old enough, they went along on the hunt. Girls, too, learned by working with their mothers. They learned to find wild foods, to prepare meals, to cure buffalo hide and deerskin, and to make clothing.

Every village had a chief to guide, rather than strongly rule over, the small group of families. Everyone in the band tried to get along. When there was a problem, the chief helped the people to find a solution. There was also a chief of the entire tribe, like the famous Chief Joseph. He inherited the position from his father, who died in 1871, and remained chief until his own death in 1904. Joseph ruled by persuading the people, not by giving orders. For

The death of Chief Joseph in 1904.

this reason, oratory (speech giving) was a very important skill among the Nez Perce and the neighboring tribes.

Throughout the year, the Nez Perce celebrated important events with special ceremonies. In spring they celebrated the Rite of the First Fruits when the first roots were ripe enough to eat. The month of May is called *Ah-Pah-Ahl*, which means "the time for digging roots." The month of August is named for the first migration of the salmon. The First Salmon Rite, like First Fruits, called for special prayers and ceremonies.

The Nez Perce enjoyed Winter Dances through the long, cold months when they spent more time in the shelter of their lodges. Each village held a Winter Dance, which lasted for three days and included lots of singing, dancing, and storytelling. Then a neighboring village had its three-day dance, and all the surrounding villages were invited. These celebrations strengthened the unity of the tribe.

Indian pictographs (or rock paintings) near the Salmon River, Idaho.

A Nez Perce baby on a cradleboard.

Key events in the life of each individual also called for special rites or ceremonies among the Nez Perce. On an infant's first birthday, the family had a big celebration and gave the child a name. When a boy reached twelve or thirteen years old, he was sent on a vision quest. Left alone on a mountaintop with no food or weapons, he would try to have a vision, or a dream, in which he would see his guardian spirit. The spirit was usually in the form of an animal or bird, and it would remain with him for life. After several days, if he had received his vision, the tired, hungry boy returned to the village and was welcomed as an adult. If he did not receive his vision, he would go out again many times until he did.

A girl coming of age also spent a month or longer away from the village. An older woman stayed with her, and they lived in a small lodge. The girl's hair was bound up in rolls. Her face was painted yellow or red, and she wore simple clothes with no decorations. She may have had a vision, but it was not required. On her last day, she sat on a hillside praying, and then she entered the village as a grown woman.

Marriage was an important rite among the Nez Perce. Family heads would often arrange the marriage. They made sure the man and woman were not related, since marriage even between distant relatives was forbidden. If both families were pleased with the match, a ceremony took place and gifts were exchanged. Divorce was allowed, but discouraged.

When a Nez Perce died, he or she was usually buried in a pit of sand or gravel marked with a pile of boulders near a river. Widows were expected to dress poorly and wail, or cry bitterly, while kneeling by the grave.

Like most Native American cultures, the Nez Perce believed in a Creator, *Hanyawat*, the God of all creation. There were also other gods, such as the gods of the sun, thunder, lightning, and wind. There was also a huge number of other spirits, including the guardian spirits seen in vision quests. It was possible for a person to have more than one guardian spirit, but never more than six. Warriors prayed to these spirits before a hunt, a battle, or another important event.

The Nez Perce also believed that some people had special

A deceased person's clothing is given away during a funeral ceremony.

healing powers. These **shamans** (SHAH-mans) were usually men, but women could also become shamans. Shamans were both healers and spiritual leaders. They skillfully treated sickness and injury with herbal medicines, sweat baths, and other methods. If the shaman decided that the illness was from natural causes, he or she would not try to heal it. However, if it was decided that the illness was caused by witchcraft or by the sick person breaking a law, then the shaman used singing, prayers, smoking, or cleansing the person with water to drive out the invading force. A successful shaman enjoyed great wealth and prestige.

A shaman's headdress.

Coyote Creates Humans

Coyote appears in the myths of many Native American cultures. He is very clever and quick-witted.

One day Coyote's friend Fox said, "Coyote, you must save the animal people. A great monster is devouring them."

Coyote decided he must kill the monster. He armed himself with knives and a pouch of pine pitch. Then he challenged the monster to swallow him, and the monster did.

Inside the monster's stomach, Coyote found the animal people. He said to them, "When I build a fire to slay the monster, he will bellow. You must then run out of every opening—mouth, nose, ears, and the part under the tail."

The animal people got ready. Coyote used his pine pitch to start a fire, the monster bellowed, and the animal people all ran out. Last of all came Coyote.

Coyote said, "This valley is so beautiful, it should have some human beings." So Coyote cut up the monster into little pieces and threw them to the north, south, east, and west. Everywhere a piece landed became a Native American tribe. Last, he created the *Nimi'ipuu*—the Nez Perce people—to take care of the beautiful valley.

A coyote's face shows its keen intelligence.

4 · A CHANGING WORLD

Until about 1850 the Nez Perce was one of the largest and most powerful tribes in the United States. They were also one of the most prosperous because of their great herds of Appaloosa horses.

This wealth and power vanished in the late 1800s, as the U.S. government forced the Nez Perce bands onto small reservations. Life was hard on the reservation, and it was harder still for the families that followed Chief Joseph in their desperate flight for freedom in Canada. Following their surrender, Chief Joseph and his people were sent to a swampy reservation in what is now Oklahoma. Many died of malaria before the government allowed most of them (except for Joseph and a few others) to return to the Idaho reservation.

So many Nez Perce died of warfare and disease that only

Nez Perce riding single file through a mountain forest.

Nez Perce board a train for the journey to their original home in Idaho.

about 1,500 remained on the reservation through the 1800s and early 1900s. They lived in poverty with almost no job opportunities, poor schools, and few doctors or health clinics. Many young people left the reservation to look for work in America's growing cities. They soon blended in with the general population.

The Nez Perce formed its own government and constitution in 1948. Beginning in the 1960s, the Nez Perce, like other tribes, sought funding from the U.S. government to improve reservation schools, health clinics, and other tribal services. In 1997 the Trust for Public Land restored to the Nez

The Nez Perce Trail

In 1968 Congress established the National Trails System, a series of recreational, scenic, and historic trails throughout the United States. Each trail provides maps, tours, and park facilities, such as campsites and restrooms. In 1986 Congress added the Nez Perce National Historic Trail to the system. The trail follows the 1877 flight of the Nez Perce from their homelands in an effort to reach freedom in Montana or Canada.

The Nez Perce National Historic Trail begins at Wallowa Lake in eastern Oregon. It winds across Idaho into Montana, through Yellowstone Park in Wyoming, and back into Montana, where it ends only 40 miles (64 km) short of the Canadian border. It travels through some of the most beautiful land in North America. To the Nez Perce, the trail is a vital part of their most sacred land.

Nez Perce leaders at the 1997 purchase of a 10,300-acre ranch in Oregon. The tribe operates the area as a wildlife refuge.

Perce more than 10,000 acres of land in northeast Oregon.

Many of the Nez Perce continue to live as their ancestors did. They raise Appaloosa horses and cattle, gather wild foods, and grow crops. Today, the Nez Perce own businesses in construction, landscaping, crafts, and computer programming, as well as gift shops and casinos. Some tribal members also have jobs outside the reservation in schools, businesses, logging, and fishing. The reservation is a pleasant community of well-maintained schools, offices, a community center, and small but comfortable homes.

The elders have the responsibility for passing Nez Perce ways on to the next generation. They teach songs and dances, and they keep alive the rich tradition of storytelling. Children are invited to attend summer camps, where they learn about the history and traditions of their tribes.

Today, like American Indians throughout the country, the Nez Perce are enjoying renewed confidence and pride in their heritage. They have restored many of the traditional celebrations, such as First Fruits and the First Salmon. The foothills of the Bitterroot Mountains are once again filled with the rhythmic beat of drums and the music of tribal chants. Dressed in their traditional headdresses and deerskin clothes, the Nez Perce welcome visitors from neighboring tribes and from nearby towns and cities. People can enjoy traditional foods and songs and gain a new appreciation for the Nez Perce way of life.

Modern Nez Perce enjoy a feast of traditional foods in a longhouse.

· TIME LINE

The Spanish introduce the first horses into North America.

The Nez Perce begin to raise horses.

American explorers Lewis and Clark visit Nez Perce lands. They are followed by fur trappers and missionaries.

The first pioneer wagon trains carrying ten thousand settlers cross Nez Perce lands.

Mid-1500s   1720s   1805   1840s

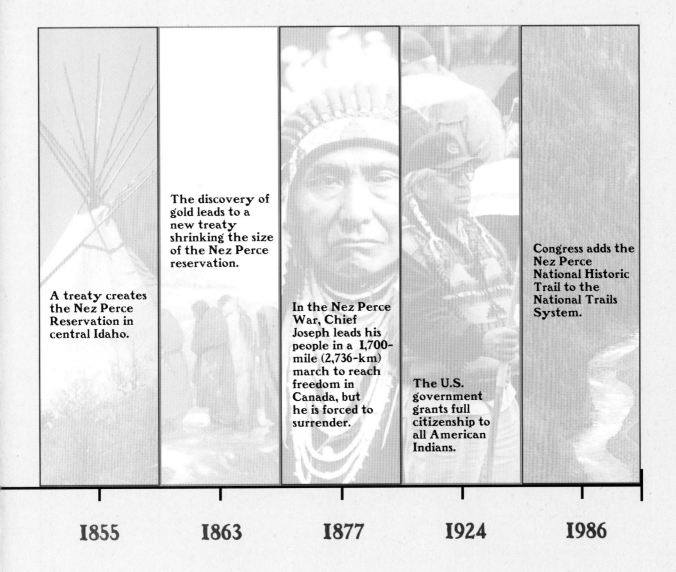

A treaty creates the Nez Perce Reservation in central Idaho.

The discovery of gold leads to a new treaty shrinking the size of the Nez Perce reservation.

In the Nez Perce War, Chief Joseph leads his people in a 1,700-mile (2,736-km) march to reach freedom in Canada, but he is forced to surrender.

The U.S. government grants full citizenship to all American Indians.

Congress adds the Nez Perce National Historic Trail to the National Trails System.

1855   1863   1877   1924   1986

GLOSSARY

Appaloosa: The breed of spotted horses carefully raised by the Nez Perce.

buckskin: The hide of a buck, or male deer, finished to a soft leather and used as clothing.

camas: The onionlike bulb of the lily plant. It was baked or boiled by the Nez Perce and tasted like a sweet potato.

couse: A root prepared as food by mashing, shaping into a small biscuit, and drying in the sun; also called biscuit root.

Great Plains: A huge area of North America where tall grasses supported enormous herds of buffalo, as well as wild horses and other animals. Most of the region is now land used for farming, as well as open range or hunting lands.

jerky: Strips of meat dried in the sun by the Nez Perce, and also dried in other ways.

pemmican: Jerky that is pounded into a powder and then mixed with berries or bone marrow and melted animal fat.

reservation: Land set aside by the U.S. government for American Indian tribes to live on.

shamans: Religious leaders responsible for Native American people's physical and spiritual well-being.

tipis (or **teepees**): Cone-shaped homes of buffalo-hunting tribes, including the Nez Perce.

travois: A sledlike carrier made of two poles tied to the shoulders of a horse or dog, used by the Nez Perce to drag heavy loads.

FIND OUT MORE

Books

King, David C. *American Kids in History: Wild West Days*. Hoboken, NJ: John Wiley & Sons, Inc., 1998.

Koestler-Grack, Rachel. *Chief Joseph*. Chicago: Heinemann Library, 2004.

Murdoch, David. *Eyewitness: North American Indian*. New York: DK Publishing, Inc., 2000.

Nerburn, Kent. *Chief Joseph & the Flight of the Nez Perce*. NY: HarperCollins, 2005.

Takacs, Stephanie. *The Nez Perce*. Danbury, CT: Children's Press, 2003.

Web Sites

Nez Perce Tribe Web Site
www.nezperce.org

About the Nez Perce
www.lewis-clarkvalley.com/indian.html

The Nez Perce National Historic Trail
www.fs.fed.us/npnht

About the Author

David C. King is an award-winning author who has written more than seventy books for children and young adults, including *The Inuit*, *The Navajo*, *The Powhatan*, and *The Sioux* in the First Americans series. He and his wife, Sharon, live in the Berkshires at the junction of New York, Massachusetts, and Connecticut. Their travels have taken them through most of the United States.

INDEX

Page numbers in **boldface** are illustrations.

maps
Flight from U.S. Troops: 1877, **15**
Homeland until the 1850s, **10**

Appaloosas. *See* horses

babies, **30**
buffalo, 7–8, **8**, 19, 23, **23**
businesses, 40

ceremonies, 29, 41, **41**
Chief Joseph, **12**, 13–14, 18, 25, **25**, 37
clothing, 7, 17, 23, **24**, 31, **32**, **36**, 41
coyote, 34, **35**
cradleboard, **30**
cultural heritage, 40–41, **41**

dances, 29, 40–41
death, **25**, 31, **32**
disease, 13, 33, 37

education, 17, 24, 38, 40–41
elders, 40
explorers, 5, 6, 9

feathers, 26
flight to freedom, 14, **15**, 37, 39, **39**

food, 7, 20–23, **23**, 29, 41, **41**
    recipe, 22

gold rush, 11–12
government
        of Nez Perce, 25, 38
        of United States, 11–13, 37, 38
Great Plains tribes, 6–7, 26

headdresses, 23, 26, **33**, 41
    project, 26–27
health care, 33, 38
homeland, 4, 5, **10**, 11–14, **15**, 18, 34, **36**, **38**, 38–40, **39**
horses, 6, 6–9, 17–19, **18**, **36**, 37
houses, 8–9, **16**, 17, 19–20, **20**, 40
hunting and fishing, 7–9, **8**, 19–20, **20**, **21**

legend, 34, **35**
lifestyle, 5, 18–19, **36**, 37–38, 40

marriage, 31
missionaries, 9, **9**
monuments, 39, **39**

names
    of horse type, 18

of individuals, 30
of Nez Perce, 5

Nez Perce War, 12–14

oratory, 25

religion, 32–33, 39, **39**
    See also missionaries
reservations, 11–13, 18, 37–38, 40
rock paintings, **28**

seasons, 8–9, 19–20, 29
shamans, 33, **33**
spirits, 30, 32
storage, 19, 20

tools and utensils, 21
trade, 9, 17
treaties, 11–12

villages, 8–9, 17, 20, 25, 29
vision quests, 30–31, 32

warfare, 7, 12–13, 32
weapons, 8, 24
wildlife refuge, **40**
women, 8, 23, 24, 31